VOGUE KNITTING

CHUNKY SCARVES & HATS™

VOGUE KNITTING

CHUNKY SCARVES & HATS™

SIXTH&SPRING BOOKS
NEW YORK

SIXTH&SPRING BOOKS
233 Spring Street
New York, New York 10013

Library of Congress Cataloging-in-Publication Data

Chunky scarves & hats
    p. cm. -- (Vogue knitting on the go!)
    ISBN 1-931543-51-8
    1. Knitting--Patterns. 2. Hats. 3. Caps (Headgear) 4. Scarves. I. Title: Chunky scarv
and hats. II. Series.

    TT825.C48 2004
    746.43'20432--dc22   2003067325

Manufactured in China

1 3 5 7 9 10 8 6 4 2

First Edition

TABLE OF CONTENTS

22 **GARTER STRIPED SCARF**
Tangerine dream

24 **HAT WITH ATTACHED SCARF**
Pippi Longstocking

26 **STRIPED HAT & SCARF**
Licorice allsorts

29 **STRIPED BERET AND SCARF**
Highland fling

34 **BELL PATTERN SCARF**
Funky chunky

36 **FAIR ISLE SCARF**
Blue diamond

38 **CABLED HAT**
Bright little braids

40 **GARTER SCARF**
Emerald isle

42 **HELMET WITH EARFLAPS**
Braveheart

44 **LACY SCARF**
Mohair magic

46 **ARAN HAT & SCARF**
Arctic ice

50 **DIAGONAL STRIPED SCARF**
Opposites attract

52 **BABY HATS**
Ice princess

54 **WOVEN SCARF**
Winter weave

57 **HAT WITH EARFLAPS**
Candy stripes

60 **EASY HAT & SCARF**
Mardi Gras

62 **RUFFLED EDGE SCARF**
Strawberry shortcake

64 **TASSELED HAT**
Blue bayou

67 **LONG SCARF**
On the fringe

70 **KID'S SCARF**
A bug's life

72 **FLOWERED SCARF**
Water lilies

74 **MEN'S GARTER-STITCHED SCARF**
Fine lines

76 **MOSAIC HAT**
Turkish tiles

79 **GARTER HAT**
Going loopy

INTRODUCTION

Chunky yarns are enjoying a resurgence in recent seasons, with their amazing textures, array of hues, and range of fibers. And their exciting characteristics translate beautifully into cozy, warm knitted garments that are perfect winterwear. Along with a fabulous look and feel, one of the best reasons for working with chunky yarns is speed.

No, chunky yarn doesn't have a built-in motor and it isn't battery run. It's simply a matter of "the thicker the yarn and the bigger the needles, the quicker the results." And for knitters who are pressed for time, need a last minute gift, or are just too impatient, chunky yarns are heaven sent; in as little as a few hours a knitter can make an amazing scarf or hat. In the world of knitting, where days and weeks of labor go into a single garment, that's like moving at the speed of light!

Keeping this in mind, we brought together the swiftest members of the knitting world: chunky yarns, and hats and scarves. Quick-knitting yarns and projects are a natural combination that serves all of those knitters who can't get enough of their craft, but can't get enough time to do it, either. In these pages you will find a selection of speedy projects for all tastes and levels, from a richly cabled scarf and fuzzy green neckwarmer, to a variegated pompom hat and a striped and tasseled cap.

So, stop reading, pull out your yarn and needles and start to **KNIT ON THE GO!**

THE BASICS

After being practiced all over the world for thousands of years, knitting is finally "in," especially with young people who are taking up the craft at a rapid rate. New and aspiring knitters are discovering the pleasure of picking up a pair of needles and a ball of yarn, and creating something warm, fashionable, unique, and handmade. With the current trend towards chunky yarns and knits, it takes no time for novices to complete accessories and then move on to more advanced projects. Chunky yarns work up swiftly and easily, which means you can have your dream sweater, scarf or hat in a fraction of the time it would normally take. You could almost call it instant gratification!

That's not to say this collection doesn't have something to offer the seasoned stitcher. As with many of our other *On the Go!* titles, we have patterns aimed at all levels, allowing new knitters to learn more with each design, and at the same time providing intermediate and advanced knitters with suitable challenges and choices. Novices may gravitate towards the vibrantly fringed Easy Hat and Scarf or the sporty Garter Striped scarf, while experienced stitchers may want to jump right in with the gorgeous Helmet Hat with Earflaps or the intricate Scottish Beret. Whatever your taste or level, the ideal chunky hat or scarf is within these pages.

SIZING

The average size of an adult scarf is 8"/20.5cm x 65"/165cm. However, there are some scarves as skinny as 4"/10cm and as long as 98"/249cm. The beauty of making a scarf is that you can make it as long or short and as wide or narrow as you want. The length can simply be determined by the amount of yarn that you have. You can easily make adjustments to our recommended measurements.

Most of the hats in this book are written in one size. Because of the stitches and yarn used, the hats have a lot of elasticity, allowing them to fit most sizes. The depth of the hat can easily be adjusted by working more or less before the top decreases. However, changing the width may be a little more difficult, particularly if there is a stitch pattern. If simple stitches are used, than adding or subtracting the number of stitches casted on is fairly simple.

CONSTRUCTION

For most basic scarf construction, cast-on the stitches for one of the shorter ends, knit the entire length, then bind off. We have

GAUGE

It is always important to knit a gauge swatch, and even more so with garments to ensure proper fit.

Patterns usually state gauge over a 4"/10cm span; however, it's beneficial to make a larger test swatch. This gives you a more precise stitch gauge, a better idea of the appearance and drape of the knitted fabric, and a chance to familiarize yourself with the stitch pattern.

The type of needles used—straight or circular, wood or metal—will influence gauge, so knit your swatch with the needles you plan to use for the project. Measure gauge as illustrated. Try different needle sizes until your sample measures the required number of stitches and rows. *To get fewer stitches to the inch/cm, use larger needles; to get more stitches to the inch/cm, use smaller needles.*

Knitting in the round may tighten the gauge, so if you measured the

gauge on a flat swatch, take another gauge reading after you begin knitting. When the piece measures at least 2"/5cm, lay it flat and measure over the stitches in the center of the piece, as the side stitches may be distorted.

It's a good idea to keep your gauge swatch in order to test blocking and cleaning methods.

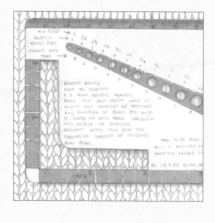

used a few other techniques, such as the Garter Striped Scarf on page 22, in which the cast-on and bound-off edges represent the length of the scarf, and the number of rows worked determines the width. It is best to use a circular needle when making a scarf in this way to easily accommodate the large number of stitches. The Bell Pattern Scarf on page 34, was made in two pieces,

then joined together at the center using the 3-needle bind-off. By working the scarf in this way, the direction of the bells will be the same while the scarf is worn.

Hats are most commonly designed from the lower edge brim and decreased to the top point. They can be worked circularly on double-pointed needles so that no seaming is necessary, or straight, with a back seam.

Categories of yarn, gauge ranges and recommended needle and hook sizes

Yarn Weight Symbol & Category Names	① Super Fine	② Fine	③ Light	④ Medium	⑤ Bulky	⑥ Super Bulky
Type of Yarns in Category	Sock, Fingering, Baby	Sport, Baby	DK, Light Worsted	Worsted, Afghan, Aran	Chunky, Craft, Rug	Super Bulky, Roving
Knit Gauge Range* in Stockinette Stitch to 4 inches	27–32 sts	23–26 sts	21–24 sts	16–20 sts	12–15 sts	6–11 sts
Recommended Needle in Metric Size Range	2.25–3.25 mm	3.25–3.75 mm	3.75–4.5 mm	4.5–5.5 mm	5.5–8 mm	9–15 mm and larger
Recommended Needle U.S. size range	1 to 3	3 to 5	5 to 7	7 to 9	9 to 11	11 to 19 and larger
Crochet Gauge* Ranges in Single Crochet to 4 inch	21–32 sts	16–20 sts	12–17 sts	11–14 sts	8–11 sts	5–9 sts
Recommended Hook in Metric Size Range	2.25–3.5 mm	3.5–4.5 mm	4.5–5.5 mm	5.5–6.5 mm	6.5–9 mm	9–12 mm and larger
Recommended Hook U.S. Size Range	B-1 to E-4	E-4 to 7	7 to I-9	I-9 to K-10½	K-10½ to M-13	M-13 to P-16 and larger

Beginner
Ideal first project.

Intermediate
For knitters with some experience. More intricate stitches, shaping and finishing.

Very Easy Very Vogue
Basic stitches, minimal shaping, simple finishing.

Experienced
For knitters able to work patterns with complicated shaping and finishing.

The Helmet with Earflaps on page 42, is worked sideways, using short rows to form the crown. The Cabled Hat on page 38 is also worked sideways, but with no crown shaping.

YARN SELECTION

For an exact reproduction of the projects shown in this book, use the yarn listed in the "Materials" section of the pattern. We've chosen yarns that are readily available in the U.S. and Canada at the time of printing. The Resources list on pages 84 and 85 provides addresses of yarn distributors. Contact them for the name of a retailer in your area.

YARN SUBSTITUTION

You may wish to substitute yarns. Perhaps you view small-scale projects as a chance to incorporate leftovers from your yarn stash, or the yarn specified may not be available in your area. You'll need to knit to the given gauge to obtain the knitted measurements with a substitute yarn (see "Gauge" on page 11). Be sure to consider how the fiber content of the substitute yarn will affect the comfort and the ease of care of your projects.

To facilitate yarn substitution, *Vogue Knitting* grades yarn by the standard stitch gauge obtained in stockinette stitch. You'll find a grading number in the "Materials" section of the pattern, immediately following the fiber type of the yarn. Look for a substitute yarn that falls into the same category. The suggested needle size and gauge on the yarn label should be comparable to that on the Standard Yarn Weight chart (see page 12).

After you've successfully gauge-swatched a substitute yarn, you'll need to figure out how much of the substitute yarn the project requires. First, find the total length of the original yarn in the pattern (multiply number of balls by yards/meters per ball). Divide this figure by the new yards/meters per ball (listed on the yarn label). Round up to the next whole number. The answer is the number of balls required.

FOLLOWING CHARTS

Charts are a convenient way to follow colorwork, lace, cable, and other stitch patterns at a glance. *Vogue Knitting* stitch charts utilize the universal knitting language of "symbolcraft." When knitting back and forth in rows, read charts from right to left on right side (RS) rows and from left to right on wrong side (WS) rows, repeating any stitch and row repeats as directed in the pattern. When knitting in the round, read charts from right to left on every round. Posting a self-adhesive note under your working row is an easy way to keep track of your place on a chart.

COLORWORK KNITTING

The Fair Isle Scarf on page 36 uses the stranding-method of colorwork. This is when motifs are closely placed, colorwork is accomplished by stranding along two or more colors per row, creating "floats" on the wrong side of the fabric. This technique is sometimes called Fair Isle knitting after

CIRCULAR NEEDLES

Hold the needle tip with the last cast-on stitch in your right hand and the tip with the first cast-on stitch in your left hand. Knit the first cast-on stitch, pulling the yarn tight to avoid a gap.

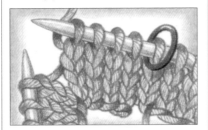

Work until you reach the marker. This completes the first round. Slip the marker to the right needle and work the next round.

TASSELS
Cut a piece of cardboard to the desired length of the tassel. Wrap yarn around the cardboard. Knot a piece of yarn tightly around one end, cut as shown, and remove the cardboard. Wrap and tie yarn around the tassel about 1"/2.5cm down from the top to secure the fringe.

DOUBLE-POINTED NEEDLES

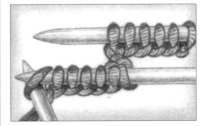

1 Cast on the required number of stitches on the first needle, plus one extra. Slip this extra stitch to the next needle as shown. Continue in this way, casting on the required number of stitches on the last needle.

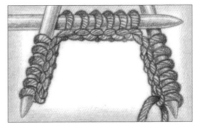

2 Arrange the needles as shown, with the cast-on edge facing the center of the triangle (or square).

3 Place a stitch marker after the last cast-on stitch. With the free needle, knit the first cast-on stitch, pulling the yarn tightly. Continue knitting in rounds, slipping the marker before beginning each round.

the traditional Fair Isle patterns that are composed of small motifs with frequent color changes.

To keep an even tension and prevent holes while knitting, pick up yarns alternately over and under one another across or around. While knitting, stretch the stitches on the needle slightly wider than the length of the float at the back to keep work from puckering.

When changing colors at the beginning of rows or rounds, carry yarn along for a few rows only, or cut yarn and rejoin when needed. It is important to keep the floats small and neat so they don't catch when pulling on the piece.

BLOCKING

Blocking is an all-important finishing step in the knitting process. It is the best way to shape pattern pieces and smooth knitted edges in preparation for sewing together or for a neat and even edge. Most items retain their shape if the blocking stages in the instructions are followed carefully. Choose a blocking method according to the yarn care label and when in doubt, test-block your gauge swatch.

Wet Block Method

Using rust-proof pins, pin pieces to measurements on a flat surface and lightly dampen using a spray bottle. Allow to dry before removing pins.

Steam Block Method

With WS facing, pin pieces. Steam lightly, holding the iron 2"/5cm above the knitting. Do not press or it will flatten stitches.

FINISHING

After blocking, there is very little, if any, finishing on a scarf. Many times, fringe is added onto the ends. You can make the fringe as short or long as you like, depending on preference or amount of leftover yarn. A crocheted edge can also be added to keep the edges from curling.

Hats have minimal or no finishing as well. If the hat was knit in the round, there is no seaming. If it is worked back and forth, or sideways, there is just one seam, usually in the back. You can always add a pompom to the top or to the end of the ties of earflaps. See the technique for making the perfect pompom on page 20.

SEWING

When using a very bulky or highly textured yarn, it is sometimes easier to seam pieces together with a finer, flat yarn. Just be sure that your sewing yarn closely matches the original yarn used in your project in color and washability.

CARE

Refer to the yarn label for the recommended cleaning method. Many of the projects in the book can be either washed by hand or in the machine on a gentle or wool cycle, in lukewarm water with a mild detergent. Do not agitate or soak for more than 10 minutes. Rinse gently with tepid water, then fold in a towel and gently squeeze the water out. Lay flat to dry away from excess heat and light. Check the yarn label for any specific care instructions such as dry cleaning or tumble drying.

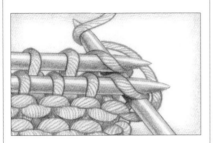

I With RS placed together, hold pieces on two parallel needles. Insert a third needle knitwise into the first stitch of each needle, and wrap the yarn around the needle as if to knit.

2 Knit these two stitches together, and slip them off the needles. *Knit the next two stitches together in the same manner.

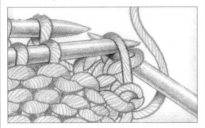

3 Slip the first stitch on the third needle over the second stitch and off the needle. Repeat from the * in Step 2 across the row until all stitches have been bound off.

The provisional cast-on, sometimes called open cast-on, is used when you want to have open stitches at the cast-on edge in order to pick up stitches later to work a hem, or if you want to weave these open stitches to the final row of stitches for a smooth seam, as in the Garter Hat on page 79. There are many different ways to work a provisional cast on, two of which are described below. The Garter Hat was worked with the crochet hook method.

With a crochet hook

I Using waste yarn of a similar weight to the project yarn and a crochet hook appropriate for that yarn, chain the number of cast-on stitches stated in the instructions. Cut a tail and pull the tail through the last chain.

2 Using the needles and working yarn, pick up one stitch through the 'purl bumps' on the back of each crochet chain. Be careful not to split the waste yarn, as this makes it difficult to pull out the crochet chain at the end.

3 Continue working pattern as described.

4 To remove waste chain, pull out the tail from the last crochet stitch. Gently and slowly pull on the tail to unravel the crochet stitches, carefully placing each released knit stitch on a needle.

Long Tail

I Leaving tails about 4"/10cm long, tie a length of scrap yarn (approximately four times the desired width) together with the main yarn in a knot. With your right hand, hold the knot on top of the needle a short distance from the tip, then place your thumb and index finger between the two yarns and hold the long ends with the other fingers. Hold your hand with your palm facing upwards and spread your thumb and index finger apart so that the yarn forms a "V" with the main yarn over your index finger and the scrap yarn over your thumb.

2 Bring the needle up through the scrap yarn loop on your thumb from front to back. Place the needle over the main yarn on your index finger and then back through the loop

on your thumb. Drop the loop off your thumb and placing your thumb back in the "V" configuration, tighten up the stitch on the needle.

3 Repeat for the desired number of stitches. The main yarn will form the stitches on the needle and the scrap yarn will make the horizontal ridge at the base of the cast-on row.

4 When picking up the stitches along the cast-on edge, carefully cut and pull out the scrap yarn as you place the exposed loops on the needle.

FRINGE

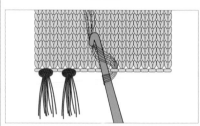

Simple fringe: Cut yarn twice desired length plus extra for knotting. On wrong side, insert hook from front to back through piece and over folded yarn. Pull yarn through. Draw ends through and tighten. Trim yarn.

Knotted fringe: After working a simple fringe (it should be longer to allow for extra knotting), take one half of the strands from each fringe and knot them with half the strands from the neighboring fringe.

TO BEGIN SEAMING

If you have left a long tail from your cast-on row, you can use this strand to begin sewing. To make a neat join at the lower edge with no gap, use the technique shown here. Thread the strand into a yarn needle. With the right sides of both pieces facing you, insert the yarn needle from back to front into the corner stitch of the piece without the tail. Making a figure eight with the yarn, insert the needle from back to front into the stitch with the cast-on tail. Tighten to close the gap.

INVISIBLE SEAMING: STOCKINETTE ST

To make an invisible side seam in a garment worked in stockinette stitch, insert the yarn needle under the horizontal bar between the first and second stitches. Insert the needle into the corresponding bar on the other piece. Pull the yarn gently until the sides meet. Continue alternating from side to side.

THE KITCHENER STITCH

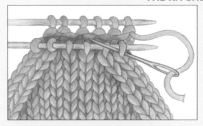

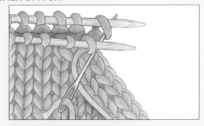

1 Insert tapestry needle purlwise (as shown) through first stitch on front needle. Pull yarn through, leaving that stitch on knitting needle.

2 Insert tapestry needle knitwise (as shown) through first stitch on back needle. Pull yarn through, leaving stitch on knitting needle.

3 Insert tapestry needle knitwise through first stitch on front needle, slip stitch off needle and insert tapestry needle purlwise (as shown) through next stitch on front needle. Pull yarn through, leaving this stitch on needle.

4 Insert tapestry needle purlwise through first stitch on back needle. Slip stitch off needle and insert tapestry needle knitwise (as shown) through next stitch on back needle. Pull yarn through, leaving this stitch on needle.
Repeat steps 3 and 4 until all stitches on both front and back needles have been grafted. Fasten off and weave in end.

 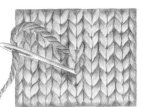 

DUPLICATE STITCH
Duplicate stitch covers a knit stitch. Bring the needle up below the stitch to be worked. Insert the needle under both loops one row above and pull it through. Insert it back into the stitch below and through the center of the next stitch in one motion, as shown.

CROCHET STITCHES

CHAIN

1 *Pass the yarn over the hook and catch it with the hook.*

2 *Draw the yarn through the loop on the hook.*

3 *Repeat steps 1 and 2 to make a chain.*

SINGLE CROCHET

1 *Insert the hook through top two loops of a stitch. Pass the yarn over the hook and draw up a loop—two loops on hook.*

2 *Pass the yarn over the hook and draw through both loops on hook.*

3 *Continue in the same way, inserting the hook into each stitch.*

HALF-DOUBLE CROCHET

1 *Pass the yarn over the hook. Insert the hook through the top two loops of a stitch.*

2 *Pass the yarn over the hook and draw up a loop—three loops on hook. Pass the yarn over the hook.*

3 *Draw through all three loops on hook.*

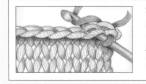

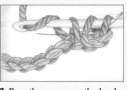

DOUBLE CROCHET

1 *Pass the yarn over the hook. Insert the hook through the top two loops of a stitch.*

2 *Pass the yarn over the hook and draw up a loop— three loops on hook.*

SLIP STITCH

Insert the crochet hook into a stitch, catch the yarn and pull up a loop. Draw the loop through the loop on the hook.

3 *Pass the yarn over the hook and draw it through the first two loops on the hook, pass the yarn over the hook and draw through the remaining two loops. Continue in the same way, inserting the hook into each stitch.*

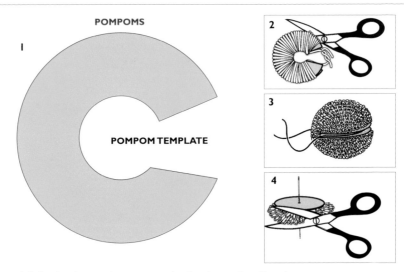

POMPOMS

POMPOM TEMPLATE

1 Following the template, cut two circular pieces of cardboard.
2 Place tie strand between the circles. Wrap yarn around circles. Cut between circles.
3 Knot tie strand tightly. Remove cardboard.
4 Place pompom between 2 smaller cardboard circles held together with a long needle and trim edges.

KNIT-ON CAST-ON

1 Make a slip knot on the left needle. *Insert the right needle knitwise into the stitch on the left needle. Wrap the yarn around the right needle as if to knit.

2 Draw the yarn through the first stitch to make a new stitch, but do not drop the stitch from the left needle.

3 Slip the new stitch to the left needle as shown. Repeat from the * until the required number of stitches is cast on.

KNITTING TERMS AND ABBREVIATIONS

approx approximately

beg begin(ning)

bind off Used to finish an edge and keep stitches from unraveling. Lift the first stitch over the second, the second over the third, etc. (UK: cast off)

cast on A foundation row of stitches placed on the needle in order to begin knitting.

CC contrast color

ch chain(s)

cm centimeter(s)

cn cable needle

cont continu(e)(ing)

dc double crochet (UK: tr-treble)

dec decrease(ing)—Reduce the stitches in a row (knit 2 together).

dpn double pointed needle(s)

foll follow(s)(ing)

g gram(s)

garter stitch Knit every row. Circular knitting: knit one round, then purl one round.

hdc half-double crochet (UK: htr-half treble)

inc increase(ing)—Add stitches in a row (knit into the front and back of a stitch).

k knit

k2tog knit 2 stitches together

lp(s) loops(s)

LH left-hand

m meter(s)

M1 make one stitch—With the needle tip, lift the strand between last stitch worked and next stitch on the left-hand needle and knit into the back of it. One stitch has been added.

MC main color

mm millimeter(s)

oz ounce(s)

p purl

p2tog purl 2 stitches together

pat pattern

pick up and knit (purl) Knit (or purl) into the loops along an edge.

pm place marker—Place or attach a loop of contrast yarn or purchased stitch marker as indicated.

rem remain(s)(ing)

rep repeat

rev St st reverse Stockinette stitch—Purl right-side rows, knit wrong-side rows. Circular knitting: purl all rounds. (UK: reverse stocking stitch)

rnd(s) round(s)

RH right-hand

RS right side(s)

sc single crochet (UK: dc - double crochet)

sk skip

SKP Slip 1, knit 1, pass slip stitch over knit 1.

SK2P Slip 1, knit 2 together, pass slip stitch over k2tog.

sl slip—An unworked stitch made by passing a stitch from the left-hand to the right-hand needle as if to purl.

sl st slip stitch (UK: single crochet)

ssk slip, slip, knit—Slip next 2 stitches knitwise, one at a time, to right-hand needle. Insert tip of left-hand needle into fronts of these stitches from left to right. Knit them together. One stitch has been decreased.

st(s) stitch(es)

St st Stockinette stitch—Knit right-side rows, purl wrong-side rows. Circular knitting: knit all rounds. (UK: stocking stitch)

tbl through back of loop

tog together

tr treble crochet (UK: dtr-double treble)

WS wrong side(s)

w&t wrap and turn

wyif with yarn in front

wyib with yarn in back

work even Continue in pattern without increasing or decreasing. (UK: work straight)

yd yard(s)

yo yarn over—Make a new stitch by wrapping the yarn over the right-hand needle. (UK: yfwd, yon, yrn)

* Repeat directions following * as many times as indicated.

[ ] Repeat directions inside brackets as many times as indicated.

GARTER STRIPED SCARF
Tangerine dream

Kristen Spurkland's unconventionally knit scarf abounds with color and texture. **Using a circular needle and garter stitch, Kristen combines dynamic red and orange furry yarns in single row stripes to create a reversible shaggy fabric.**

KNITTED MEASUREMENTS
■ Approx 5" x 40"/12.5 x 101.5cm

MATERIALS
■ 1 1¾oz/50g ball each (each approx 72yd/65m) of Gedifra/KFI *Micro Chic* (acrylic) in #3342 red (A) and #3321 orange (B) **⑤**
■ Size 10 (6mm) circular needle, 16"/40cm long *or size to obtain gauge*

GAUGE
15 sts and 26 rows to 4"/10cm over garter st using size 10 (6mm) needles.
Take time to check gauge.

SCARF
With A, cast on 19 sts. Turn work (to use other end of needle). ***Row I (RS)** With B, knit. Slide work to other end of needle so that A is in position to work next row on RS. **Row 2 (RS)** With A, purl. Turn work. **Row 3 (WS)** With B, purl. Slide work to other end of needle so that A is in position to work next row on WS. **Row 4 (WS)** With A, knit. Turn work. Rep from * until both balls of yarn are used. Bind off on row 3.

Irina Poludnenko channels the long-haired fairy tale heroine with this dual-function hat that will insure that you never lose your winter accessories again. A ribbed watchcap is attached to two cabled ends to make a convenient scarf or, if you like, faux braids.

SIZES
One size fits all.

KNITTED MEASUREMENTS
- Head circumference 16"/40.5cm
- Depth 8"/20.5cm
- Earflap length 30"/76cm

MATERIALS
- 2 4oz/113g balls (each approx 125yd/114m) of Brown Sheep Yarn Co. *Lamb's Pride Bulky* (wool/mohair) in #M77 blue **(5)**
- 1 pair size 10½ (6.5mm) needles *or size to obtain gauge*
- Cable needle
- Stitch holders

GAUGE
12 sts and 14 rows to 4"/10cm over pat st using size 10½ (6.5mm) needles.
Take time to check gauge.

CABLE PATTERN
(over 15 sts)
Row 1 (RS) K2, p1, k9, p1, k2.
Rows 2, 4, 6 and 8 K1, p1, k1, p9, k1, p1, k1.
Row 3 Rep row 1.

Row 5 K2, p1, k3, 6-st RC (sl 3 sts to cn and hold to *back*, k3, k3 from cn), p1, k2.
Row 7 K2, p1, 6-st RC, k3, p1, k2.
Rep rows 1-8 for cable pat.

SCARF
(make 2 pieces)
Cast on 30 sts. Work in k1, p1 rib for 5"/12.5cm. **Next row (RS)** K2tog across—15 sts. Work in cable pat until piece measures 32"/81cm from beg. Place sts on holder.

HAT
Cast on 8 sts, k across 15 sts from first holder, cast on 16 sts, k across 15 sts from second holder, cast on 9 sts—63 sts. Work in k1, p1 rib over all sts as foll: **Row 1 (WS)** K1, *p1, k1; rep from * to last st, k1. **Row 2** K2, *p1, k1; rep from * to last 2 sts, k2. Rep rows 1 and 2 for rib until hat measures 4"/10cm.
Shape top
Next row (RS) K2, p1, *pm, [k1, p1] 5 times; rep from * 5 times more, work to end. Work 1 row even. **Next (dec) row (RS)** *Work to marker, sl marker, SK2P; rep from * to end—51 sts. Work 3 rows even. Rep last 4 rows (12 sts dec'd every dec row) 3 times more—15 sts. **Last (dec) row** K1, *k2tog; rep from * to end—8 sts. Cut yarn, leaving approx 12"/30.5cm long tail. Draw through rem sts and fasten tightly. Sew side seam.

STRIPED HAT & SCARF
Licorice allsorts

Classic black-and-white stripes get a new look in this design from Lois Young. Every fourth row features a nontraditional stripe of aqua, while matching tassels on each end create a dynamic burst of color. The matching four-tasseled hat in vertical stripes adds offbeat style.

SIZES
Hat
One size fits all.

KNITTED MEASUREMENTS
Hat
- Head circumference 17"/43cm (unstretched)
- Depth 8½"/21.5cm

Scarf
- Approx 8" x 55"/20.5 x 139.5cm (without fringe)

MATERIALS
- 5 1¾oz/50g balls (each approx 64yd/58m) of Anny Blatt *Rustique* (wool) in #383 black (MC) **(4)**
- 3 balls each in #182 ecru (A) and #156 aqua (B)
- One pair each sizes 8 and 9 (5 and 5.5mm) needles *or size to obtain gauge*
- Size G/6 (4mm) crochet hook

GAUGES
Hat
16 sts and 30 rows to 4"/10cm over garter st using size 8 (5mm) needles.
Scarf
15 sts and 28 rows to 4"/10cm over garter st using size 9 (5.5mm) needles.
Take time to check gauges.

GARTER STITCH PATTERN
Row 1 (RS) Sl 1 purlwise, k to end.
Row 2 Sl 1 purlwise, k to last st, k1 in color of next ridge.
Rep these 2 rows for garter st pat.

HAT STRIPE PATTERN
2 rows each of A, MC, B, MC, A, MC, A, MC.
Rep these 16 rows for stripe pat.

SCARF STRIPE PATTERN
2 rows each of MC, A, MC, A, MC, A, MC, B.
Rep these 16 rows for stripe pat.

Notes
1 Hat is knit sideways in one piece.
2 Carry colors along side of piece, with the exception of color B in the scarf.

HAT
With size 8 (5mm) needles and MC, cast on 33 sts. Work 16 rows hat stripe pat 8 times. Bind off on last WS row.

FINISHING
Sew cast-on edge to bound-off edge. Sew 4 points of hat as foll: Using edge where

colors have been carried, fold along a color B ridge. Sew sides of fold together, stopping at next pair of color B ridges. Rep fold at next color B ridge until all 4 points have been sewn.

With B, make four 5"/12.5cm tassels. Sew to points.

SCARF

With size 9 (5.5mm) needles and B, cast on 30 sts. Work 16 rows scarf stripe pat 24 times. Bind off on last WS row.

Fringe

Cut 12"/30.5cm lengths of B. With crochet hook, attach 1 fringe in each st of cast-on and bound-off edges.

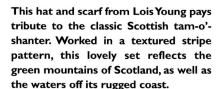

This hat and scarf from Lois Young pays tribute to the classic Scottish tam-o'-shanter. Worked in a textured stripe pattern, this lovely set reflects the green mountains of Scotland, as well as the waters off its rugged coast.

SIZES

Beret

One size fits all. This beret is a loose-fitting style.

KNITTED MEASUREMENTS

Scarf

- Approx 8" x 56"/20.5 x 142cm (without fringe)

Beret

- Head circumference approx 23"/58.5cm

MATERIALS

- 2 3½oz/100g balls (each approx 138yd/126m) of Manos Del Uruguay/Design Source *Manos* (wool) in color A blue (A)
- 1 ball each in color C light blue (B) and #55 olive green (C) (4)
- Size 10 (6mm) circular needle, 24"/60cm long *or size to obtain gauge*
- One set size 10 (6mm) dpn
- Size G/6 (4mm) crochet hook
- Stitch markers

GAUGE

15 sts and 24 rows to 4"/10cm over textured stripe pat using size 10 (6mm) needles.
Take time to check gauge.

Notes

1 The first and last st of every row is worked in a St st/slip st selvage over 2 rows as foll: **Row 1** K the selvage st on RS rows and p the selvage st on WS rows. **Row 2** Slip the selvage st wyib on RS rows and wyif on WS rows. Rep rows 1 and 2 for St st/slip st selvage. This creates a chain-like selvage at the edge and prevents the work from curling.

2 Selvage sts are not included in textured stripe pat instructions.

3 When working beret, change to dpn when hat circumference becomes too small for circular needle.

TEXTURED STRIPE PATTERN

(over an odd number of sts)

Row 1 (WS) With A, purl.

Row 2 *With A, k1, p1; rep from *, end k1.

Row 3 *With B, p1, with A, p1; rep from *, end p1 with B.

Row 4 With A, knit. Slide sts to other end of needle.

Row 5 (RS) With B, purl.

Row 6 *With B, p1, k1; rep from *, end p1.

Row 7 *With C, k1, with B, k1; rep from *, end k1 with C.

Row 8 With B, knit. Slide sts to other end of needle.

Row 9 (WS) With C, purl.

Row 10 *With C, k1, p1; rep from *, end k1 with C.

Row 11 *With A, p1, with C, p1; rep from

*, end p1 with A.

Row 12 With A, purl.

Row 13 *With A, p1, k1; rep from * end p1.

Row 14 With A, knit.

Row 15 *With B, p1, with A, p1; rep from * end p1 with B.

Row 16 With A, purl. Slide sts to other end of needle.

Row 17 (RS) *With B, k1, p1; rep from *, end k1 with B.

Row 18 With B, purl.

Row 19 *With C, k1, with B k1; rep from *, end k1 with C.

Row 20 With B, purl. Slide sts to other end of needle.

Row 21 (WS) With C, knit.

Row 22 *With C, k1, p1; rep from *, end k1 with C.

Row 23 *With A, p1, with C, p1; rep from *, end p1 with A.

Row 24 With C, purl. Slide sts to other end of needle.

Row 25 (RS) With A, knit.

Row 26 *With A, p1, k1; rep from *, end p1.

Row 27 *With B, k1, with A, k1; rep from *, end k1 with B.

Row 28 With A, purl. Slide sts to other end of needle.

Row 29 (WS) With B, knit.

Row 30 *With B, k1, p1; rep from *, end k1.

Row 31 *With C, p1, with B, p1; rep from *, end p1 with C.

Row 32 With B, p. Slide sts to other end of needle.

Row 33 (RS) With C, knit.

Row 34 *With C, p1, k1; rep from *, end p1 with C.

Row 35 *With A, k1, with C, k1; rep from *, end k1 with A.

Row 36 With A, knit.

Row 37 *With A, k1, p1; rep from * end k1.

Row 38 With A, purl.

Row 39 *With B, k1, with A, k1; rep from * end k1 with B.

Row 40 With A, knit. Slide sts to other end of needle.

Row 41 (WS) *With B, p1, k1; rep from *, end p1 with B.

Row 42 With B, knit.

Row 43 *With C, p1, with B p1; rep from *, end p1 with C.

Row 44 With B, knit. Slide sts to other end of needle.

Row 45 (RS) With C, purl.

Row 46 *With C, p1, k1; rep from *, end p1 with C.

Row 47 *With A, k1, with C, k1; rep from *, end k1 with A.

Row 48 With C, knit. Slide sts to other end of needle.

Rep rows 1-48 for textured stripe pat.

SCARF

With A, cast on 31 sts. Work 48 rows of textured stripe pat 7 times. Work rows 1 and 2 once more. Bind off knitwise on WS with A.

FRINGE

Cut 13"/33cm lengths of A. With crochet hook, use 2 strands of yarn for each fringe, placing fringe in each cast on and bind off st.

BERET

With A, cast on 72 sts. Pm and join, being careful not to twist sts.

Border

Work in k1, p1 rib for 6 rnds. P next rnd on RS for turning ridge. Work in p1, k1 rib for 7 rnds.

Beg textured stripe pat

Inc rnd *K3, M1; rep from * around—96 sts.

Rnd 1 *With B, k1, with A, k1; rep from * around.

Rnd 2 With A, knit.

Rnd 3 With B, purl.

Rnd 4 *With B, k1, p1; rep from * around.

Rnd 5 *With C, k1, with B, k1; rep from * around.

Rnd 6 With B, purl.

Rnd 7 With C, knit.

Rnd 8 *With C, k1, p1; rep from * around.

Rnd 9 *With A, k1, with C, k1; rep from * around.

Rnd 10 With A, purl.

Rnd 11 *With A, k1, p1; rep from * around.

Rnd 12 With A, knit.

Rnd 13 *With B, k1, with A, k1; rep from * around.

Rnd 14 With A, purl.

Rnd 15 *With B, k1, p1; rep from * around.

Rnd 16 With B, knit.

Rnd 17 *With C, k1, with B, k1; rep from * around.

Rnd 18 With B, knit.

Rnd 19 With C, purl.

Rnd 20 *With C, k1, p1; rep from * around.

Rnd 21 *With A, k1, with C, k1; rep from * around.

Rnd 22 With C, purl.

Rnd 23 *With A, k10, k2tog; rep from * around—88 sts.

Rnd 24 *With A, k1, p1; rep from * around.

Rnd 25 *[With B, k1, with A, k1] 4 times, with B, k1, with A, k2tog; rep from * around—80 sts.

Rnd 26 With A, knit.

Rnd 27 *With B, p8, p2tog; rep from * around—72 sts.

Rnd 28 *With B, k1, p1; rep from * around.

Rnd 29 *[With C, k1, with B, k1] 3 times, with C, k1, with B, k2tog; rep from * around—64 sts.

Rnd 30 With B, purl.

Rnd 31 *With C, k6, k2tog; rep from * around—56 sts.

Rnd 32 *With C, k1, p1; rep from *around.

Rnd 33 *[With A, k1, with C, k1] twice,

with A, k1, with C, k2tog; rep from * around—48 sts.

Rnd 34 *With A, p4, p2tog; rep from * around—40 sts.

Rnd 35 *With A, k1, p1, k1, p2tog; rep from * around—32 sts.

Rnd 36 *With A, k2, k2tog; rep from * around—24 sts.

Rnd 37 *With B, k1, with A, k2tog; rep from * around—16 sts.

Rnd 38 *With A, k2tog; rep from * around—8 sts.

Cut yarn, leaving 6"/15cm of yarn. Draw through loops of rem sts and fasten off. Fold border at turning ridge to WS and sew to inside of hat.

With B, make a 2"/5cm pompom and tie to top of hat.

BELL PATTERN SCARF
Funky chunky

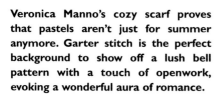

Veronica Manno's cozy scarf proves that pastels aren't just for summer anymore. Garter stitch is the perfect background to show off a lush bell pattern with a touch of openwork, evoking a wonderful aura of romance.

KNITTED MEASUREMENTS

■ Approx 11½" x 52"/29 x 132cm

MATERIALS

■ 5 3½oz/100g balls (each approx 60yd/55m) of Tahki Yarns/Tahki•Stacy Charles, Inc. *Baby* (wool) in #4 pink **(6)**
■ One pair size 15 (10mm) needles *or size to obtain gauge*
■ Stitch holders

GAUGE

8 sts and 14 rows to 4"/10cm over pat st using size 15 (10mm) needles.
Take time to check gauge.

PATTERN STITCH

(multiple of 9 sts plus 5)
Note St count varies on each row. Count sts after row 8 only.
Row 1 (RS) K3, *yo, k8, yo, k1; rep from * to last 2 sts, k2.
Row 2 K4, *p8, k3; rep from * to last st, k1.
Row 3 K4, *yo, k8, yo, k3; rep from * to last st, k1.
Row 4 K5, *p8, k5; rep from * to end.
Row 5 K5, *yo, k8, yo, k5; rep from * to end.
Row 6 K6, *yo, p8, k7; rep from *, end k6.
Row 7 K6, *k4tog tbl, k4tog, k7; rep from *, end k6.
Row 8 Knit.
Rep rows 1-8 for pat st.

Note

Scarf is worked in two pieces then joined together at the center.

SCARF

Cast on 23 sts.
First piece
Work 8 rows of pat st 11 times. Place sts on holder. Work 2nd piece same as first.

FINISHING

Block pieces to measurements.
With RS facing, work 3-needle bind off to join the two pieces.

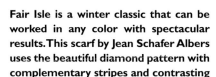

Fair Isle is a winter classic that can be worked in any color with spectacular results. This scarf by Jean Schafer Albers uses the beautiful diamond pattern with complementary stripes and contrasting blues for a warm style with a cool look.

KNITTED MEASUREMENTS

- Approx 8½" x 75"/21.5 x 190.5cm

MATERIALS

- 3 3½oz/100g balls (each approx 127yd/117m) of Classic Elite Yarns *Montera* (wool/llama) in #3848 dk blue (MC)
- 1 ball in #3830 lt blue (A)
- One pair size 9 (5.5mm) needles *or size to obtain gauge*
- Size F/5 (3.75mm) crochet hook

GAUGE

16 sts and 21 rows to 4"/10cm over St st using size 9 (5.5mm) needles.
Take time to check gauge.

SCARF

With MC, cast on 31 sts. Work in St st for 4 rows. Cont in St st (except as noted on chart) as work as foll:

Beg chart

[Work 10-st rep of chart 3 times, then work first st once more. Cont as established, through chart row 33. Cont in St st and MC for 4"/10cm, end with a WS row] twice. Work 32 rows of chart. Cont in St st and MC for 18"/45.5cm. Rep from

* to * once. Cont in St st and MC for 4 rows. Bind off.

FINISHING

Block to measurements.

Fringe

Cut 8"/20.5cm strands of A. With crochet hook, attach 1 strand in each st along edges of scarf.

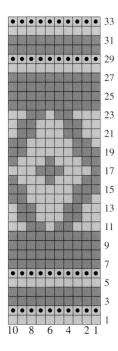

Color and Stitch Key

- ☐ K on RS, p on WS with A
- ☐ K on RS, p on WS with MC
- ☐● K on WS with A

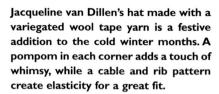

Jacqueline van Dillen's hat made with a variegated wool tape yarn is a festive addition to the cold winter months. A pompom in each corner adds a touch of whimsy, while a cable and rib pattern create elasticity for a great fit.

SIZES
One size fits all. This hat is a loose-fitting style.

KNITTED MEASUREMENTS
- Head circumference 20"/51cm
- Depth 8"/20.5cm

MATERIALS
- 4 1¾oz/50g balls (each approx 76yd/70m) of Artful Yarns/JCA *Vaudeville* (wool) in #13 red **(5)**
- One pair size 11 (8mm) needles *or size to obtain gauge*

GAUGE
27 sts and 21 rows to 4"/10cm over chart pat using size 11 (8mm) needles.
Take time to check gauge.

STITCH GLOSSARY
4-st RC Sl 2 sts to cn and hold to *back*, k2, k2 from cn.

4-st LC Sl 2 sts to cn and hold to *front*, k2, k2 from cn.

6-st RPC Sl 4 sts to cn and hold to *back*, k2, then p2, k2 from cn.

6-st LPC Sl 2 sts to cn and hold to *front*, k2, p2, then k2 from cn.

Note
Hat is worked sideways in one piece.

HAT
Cast on 54 sts. **Preparation row (WS)** K2, *[p2, k2] 4 times, p2, k1, p6, k1; rep from * to end.

Beg chart
Row I (RS) Beg with st 1, work 26-st rep of chart twice, p2. **Row 2** K2, work 26-st rep of chart twice. Cont in pat as established, working 4 rows of chart until piece measures 20"/51cm from beg. Bind off.

FINISHING
Fold hat in thirds, so then cast-on edge meets bound-off edge. Sew together to form back seam. Sew right edges together to form top seam.

Make 2 pompoms and sew to top corners of hat.

26-st rep

Stitch Key
☐ K on RS, p on WS

⊟ P on RS, k on WS

▷◁ 4-st RC

▷◁ 4-st LC

◁ 6-st LPC

▷ 6-st RPC

GARTER SCARF

Emerald isle

Fuzzy, green and unique, this neckwarmer from designer Jean Guirguis is marvelously simple, with a slot that holds the ends of the scarf in place for maximum warmth. Just knit up in garter stitch and let the yarn do all the work.

KNITTED MEASUREMENTS
■ Approx 10" x 38"/25.5 x 96.5cm

MATERIALS
■ 1 6½oz/200g ball (approx 88yd/80m) of Skacel Collection *No Kidding* (acrylic) in #75 dk green (⑥)
■ One pair size 15 (10mm) needles *or size to obtain gauge*

GAUGE
11 sts and 14 rows to 4"/10cm over garter st using size 15 (10mm) needles.
Take time to check gauge.

SCARF
Cast on 28 sts. Work in garter st until piece measures 8"/20.5cm from beg. **Next row (RS)** Work 10 sts, bind off center 8 sts, work to end. **Next row** Work 10 sts, cast on 8 sts over bound-off sts, work to end. Cont in garter st until piece measures 38"/96.5cm from beg. Bind off. Make 4 pompoms and attach to each corner.

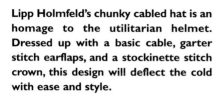

Lipp Holmfeld's chunky cabled hat is an homage to the utilitarian helmet. Dressed up with a basic cable, garter stitch earflaps, and a stockinette stitch crown, this design will deflect the cold with ease and style.

SIZES
One size fits all. This hat is a loose fitting style.

KNITTED MEASUREMENTS
- Head circumference 21"/53cm
- Depth 9"/23cm

MATERIALS
- 1 8oz/250g ball (approx 132yd/121m) of Brown Sheep Yarn Co. *Burly Spun* (wool) in #BS181 red (6)
- One pair size 15 (10mm) needles *or size to obtain gauge*
- Size K/10½ (6.5mm) crochet hook
- Cable needle

GAUGE
8 sts and 12 rows to 4"/10cm over St st using size 15 (10mm) needles.
Take time to check gauge.

STITCH PATTERN
(over 28 sts)
Row 1 (RS) K2, p2, k6, p2, k2, p1, k13.

Row 2 K14, p2, k2, p6, k2, p2.
Row 3 K2, p2, k6, p2, k2, p1, k11, turn.
Row 4 P11, k1, p2, k2, p6, k2, p2.
Row 5 K2, p2, sl next 3 sts to cn and hold to *back*, k3, k3 from cn, p2, k2, p1, k9, turn.
Row 6 P9, k1, p2, k2, p6, k2, p2.
Row 7 K2, p2, k6, p2, k2, p1, k7, turn.
Row 8 P7, k1, p2, k2, p6, k2, p2.
Rep rows 1-8 for st pat.

HAT
Cast on 28 sts. Beg with row 3, work 8 rows of st pat 8 times. Bind off knitwise.

FINISHING
Sew cast-on and bound-off edges tog for back seam.
Ear flaps
With WS facing, beg 8 sts from back seam, pick up and k10 sts along side of hat. Work in garter st for 10 rows. **Next row (RS)** Dec 1 st at beg of this row, then *every* row 5 times more—4 sts. **Next row (RS)** K2tog, k2. **Next row** K2tog, k1. **Next row** K2tog. Insert crochet hook in last st and ch 30, turn. Sl st in each ch. Work 10 sl sts into side of flap. Cut yarn, leaving 20"/51cm, thread through back of flap and work 10 sl sts down other side of flap. Fasten off.
Work a 2nd ear flap in same way along other side of back seam.

LACY SCARF
Mohair magic

J.P. Hornicek takes advantage of mohair's soft and sensual traits with this beautiful lace and cable pattern. The openwork design is feminine, fashionable and remarkably warm—an ideal accessory.

KNITTED MEASUREMENTS
■ Approx 9½" x 64"/24 x 162.5cm

MATERIALS
■ 1 3½oz/100g skein (approx 189yd/175m) of Colinette Yarn/Unique Kolours *Mohair* (mohair) in #66 mist (**5**)
■ One pair size 10½ (6.5mm) needles *or size to obtain gauge*
■ Cable needle

GAUGE
12 sts and 16 rows to 4"/10cm over lace and cable pat using size 10½ (6.5mm) needles.
Take time to check gauge.

LACE AND CABLE PATTERN
Row 1 (RS) Sl 1, p1, yo, SKP, yo, p1, k1, [yo, k2tog] twice, 6-st LC (sl 3 sts to cn and hold to *front*, k3, k3 from cn), [yo, k2tog] twice, k1, p1, yo, SKP, yo, p1, k1.
Row 2 and all WS rows Sl 1, k1, p3, k1, p16, k1, p3, k2.
Rows 3 and 11 Sl 1, p1, k3, p1, k1, [k2tog, yo] twice, k6, [k2tog, yo] twice, k1, p1, k3, p1, k1.
Rows 5 and 9 Sl 1, p1, k3, p1, k1, [yo, k2tog] twice, k6, [yo, k2tog] twice, k1, p1, k3, p1, k1.
Row 7 Sl 1, p1, yo, SKP, yo, p1, k1, [k2tog, yo] twice, 6-st LC, [k2tog, yo] twice, k1, p1, yo, SKP, yo, p1, k1.
Row 12 Rep row 2.
Rep rows 1-12 for lace and cable pat.

Note
Sl st knitwise when working SKP in rows 1 and 7 of lace and cable pat. On all other rows, sl st purlwise.

SCARF
Using knitted cast on method, loosely cast on 28 sts.
Preparation row 1 (RS) K1, p1, k3, p1, k16, p1, k3, p1, k1.
Preparation row 2 Sl 1, k1, p3, k1, p16, k1, p3, k2.
Work in lace and cable pat until piece measures 64"/162.5cm, end with a RS row. Bind off loosely.

FINISHING
Block lightly to measurements.

ARAN HAT & SCARF
Arctic ice

■■■▢

Ice blue is just the color to capture the essence of winter chill. Designer Gayle Bunn also uses it to create an exceptionally warm scarf worked in traditional cables and diamond cables with seed stitch borders. A matching hat with pompom makes this set the epitome of timeless winter style.

Hat
One size fits all. This hat is a standard fitting style.

KNITTED MEASUREMENTS
Hat
■ Head circumference 16"/40.5cm (unstretched)
■ Depth 8"/20.5cm
Scarf
■ Approx 9½" x 61"/24 x 155cm

MATERIALS
Hat
■ 2 3½oz/100g balls (each approx 78yd/71m) of Patons® *Up Country* (wool) in #80953 lt blue ⑤
Scarf
■ 5 balls in #80953 lt blue
Both
■ One pair size 10½ (6.5mm) needles *or size to obtain gauge*
■ Cable needle

GAUGE
12 sts and 22 rows to 4"/10cm over seed st using size 10½ (6.5mm) needles.
Take time to check gauge.

SEED STITCH
Row 1 (RS) *P1, k1; rep from * to end.
Row 2 K the purl sts and p the knit sts.
Rep row 2 for seed st.

STITCH GLOSSARY
2-st BPC Sl 1 st to cn and hold to *back*, k1tbl, p1 from cn.
2-st FPC Sl 1 st to cn and hold to *front*, p1, k1tbl from cn.
3-st BC Sl 1 st to cn and hold to *back*, k2, k1 from cn.
3-st FC Sl 2 sts to cn and hold to *front*, k1, k2 from cn.
3-st BPC Sl 1 st to cn and hold to *back*, k2, p1 from cn.
3-st FPC Sl 2 sts to cn and hold to *front*, p1, k2 from cn.
4-st FC Sl 2 sts to cn and hold to *front*, k2, k2 from cn.
6-st BC Sl 3 sts to cn and hold to *back*, k3, k3 from cn.
6-st FC Sl 3 sts to cn and hold to *front*, k3, k3 from cn.

HAT
Cast on 62 sts. **Row 1 (RS)** *K2, p2; rep from *, end k2. **Row 2** *P2, k2; rep from *, end p2. Rep rows 1 and 2 for k2, p2 rib until piece measures 4½"/11.5cm from beg, inc 8 sts evenly across last WS row—70 sts.
Beg charts
Row 1 (RS) Work seed st over 13 sts, p2, k1tbl, p2, work row 1 of cable chart A over next 6 sts, p2, k1tbl, work row 1 of diamond chart over next 16 sts, k1tbl, p2,

work row 1 of cable chart B over next 6 sts, p2, k1tbl, p2, work seed st over 13 sts.

Row 2 Work seed st over 13 sts, k2, p1tbl, k2, work row 2 of cable chart B over next 6 sts, k2, p1tbl, work row 2 of diamond chart over next 16 sts, p1tbl, k2, work row 2 of cable chart A over next 6 sts, k2, p1tbl, k2, work seed st over 13 sts.

Cont in pats as established through diamond chart row 22, then work rows 1 and 2 once more.

Shape top

Row 1 (RS) P1, k1, [p3tog, k1] twice, p3tog, p2tog, k1tbl, p2tog, k6, p2tog, k1tbl, p2tog, cont next 12 sts in diamond pat, p2tog, k1tbl, p2tog, k6, p2tog, k1tbl, p2tog, [p3tog, k1] 3 times, p1—50 sts.

Work 1 row even.

Row 3 [P1, k1] 3 times, p2, k1tbl, p1, 6-st BC, p1, k1tbl, p2tog, cont next 10 sts in diamond pat, p2tog, k1tbl, p1, 6-st FC, p1, k1tbl, p2, [k1, p1] 3 times—48 sts.

DIAMOND CHART

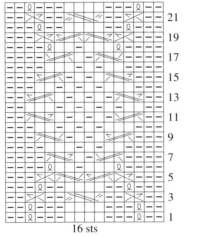

16 sts

CABLE CHART A

6 sts

CABLE CHART B

6 sts

Stitch Key

☐ K on RS, p on WS

⊟ P on RS, k on WS

 Q K1 tb1 on RS, P1 tb1 on WS

⬚ 2-st FPC

⬚ 2-st RPC

⬚ 3-st FC

⬚ 3-st BC

⬚ 3-st FPC

⬚ 3-st BPC

⬚ 4-st FC

⬚ 6-st FC

⬚ 6-st BC

Row 4 [P1, k1] 4 times, p1tbl, k1, [p2tog] 3 times, k1, p1tbl, k2, p1tbl, p2tog, p1, k1, p2tog, p1tbl, k2, p1tbl, k1, [p2tog] 3 times, k1, p1tbl, [k1, p1] 4 times—40 sts.
Row 5 P1, k1, p3tog, k1, p2, k1tbl, p1, k3, p1, k1tbl, p2tog, k2tog, k1, p1, k2tog, p2tog, k1tbl, p1, k3, p1, k1tbl, p2, k1, p3tog, k1, p1—32 sts.
Row 6 [P1, k1] 3 times, p1tbl, k1, p3tog, k1, p1tbl, k1, [p2tog] twice, k1, p1tbl, k1, p3tog, k1, p1tbl, [k1, p1] 3 times—26 sts.
Cut yarn, leave a long end. Draw through rem sts and fasten tightly. Sew center back seam, reversing seam for turnback cuff. Make large pompom and attach to top of hat.

SCARF

Cast on 31 sts. **Row 1 (RS)** *K1, p1; rep from * to last st, k1. Rep last row for seed st 7 times more, inc 9 sts evenly across last WS row—40 sts.

Beg charts
Row 1 (RS) Work 2 sts in seed st, p1, work row 1 of cable chart A over next 6 sts, p2, k1tbl, work row 1 of diamond chart over next 16 sts, k1tbl, p2, work row 1 of cable chart B across next 6 sts, p1, work 2 sts in seed st.

Row 2 Work 2 sts in seed st, k1, work row 2 of cable chart B across next 6 sts, k2, p1tbl, work row 2 of diamond chart over next 16 sts, p1tbl, k2, work row 2 of cable chart A across next 6 sts, k1, work 2 sts in seed st.

Cont in pats as established until piece measures 59½"/151cm from beg, end with row 2 of diamond chart, dec 9 sts evenly across last row—31 sts. Work 8 rows seed st. Bind off in pat.

DIAGONAL STRIPED SCARF

Opposites attract

Irina Poludnenko designed this sophisticated scarf in the urbanite's color palette: black and white. Diagonal stripes draw your eyes to the jagged edges, and seed stitch creates a lovely reversible texture.

KNITTED MEASUREMENTS
- Approx 7" x 92"/18 x 233.5cm

MATERIALS
- 2 4oz/125g balls (each approx 130yd/120m) of Fiesta Yarns *Kokopelli* (mohair/wool) in #k01black (A)
- 2 balls in #k02white (B)
- One pair size 10 (6mm) needles *or size to obtain gauge*

GAUGE
14 sts and 24 rows to 4"/10cm over seed st using size 10 (6mm) needles.
Take time to check gauge.

SEED STITCH
Row 1 (RS) *K1, p1; rep from * to end.
Row 2 K the purl sts and p the knit sts.
Rep row 2 for seed st.

SCARF
With A, cast on 28 sts. *Work in seed st for 18 rows. **Next row (RS)** Bind off 7 sts. Cut yarn and join B. Work to end, cast on 7 sts. Rep from * 20 times more, alternating A and B (21 color blocks). Bind off.

Ice princess

The winter cap gets dressed up in this Michelle Woodford design. Knitted in powdery pastels and trimmed with white novelty faux-fur yarn, these stockinette stitched hats are a sweet addition to any child's wardrobe.

SIZES

Instructions are written for Infant's size 0-3 months. Changes for sizes 6 months and 12-18 months are in parentheses. Shown in all three sizes. This cap is a close-fitting style.

KNITTED MEASUREMENTS

- Head circumference 12½ (15, 17)"/32 (38, 43)cm
- Depth 6 (7, 8)"/15 (18, 20.5)cm

MATERIALS

All hats

- 1 1¾oz/50g ball (approx 55yd/50m) of Berroco, Inc. *Pronto* (cotton/acrylic) in #4430 lime or #4425 lilac or #4483 pink (MC) (5)
- 1 1¾oz/50g ball (approx 50yd/ 45m) of Berroco, Inc. *Zap* (polyester) in #3501 white (A) (5)
- 1 1¾oz/50g ball (approx 90yd/ 83m) of Berroco, Inc. *Furz* (nylon/wool/ acrylic) in #3801 white (B) (4)
- One set (4) size 9 (5.5mm) dpn *or size to obtain gauge*
- Stitch markers

GAUGE

13 sts and 18 rows to 4"/10cm over St st with MC using size 9 (5.5mm) dpn.
Take time to check gauge.

DOUBLE VERTICAL DECREASE (DV DEC)

Insert RH needle into the next 2 sts on LH needle one at a time as if to K. Sl them to the RH needle (sts are twisted). Return 2 sl sts to LH needle, keeping them twisted. Insert the RH needle through the back loops of the second and first sl sts and sl them together off the LH needle. P the next st. With the LH needle, pass the 2 sl sts over the p st and off the RH needle.

Note

Use 1 strand of A and B held tog for brim.

HAT

With A and B held tog, cast on 40 (48, 56) sts. Divide sts evenly over 3 needles. Pm for beg of rnd.
Rnd 1 Purl. **Rnd 2** Knit. Rep last 2 rnds twice more. P 1 rnd. Change to MC and work in St st until MC measures 2½ (3, 3½)"/6.5 (7.5, 10)cm

Shape crown
Next (dec) rnd *K7 (9, 11) sts, dv-dec; rep from * around—32 (40, 48) sts. Work 1 rnd even. **Next (dec) rnd** *K5 (7, 9), dv-dec; rep from * around—24 (32, 40) sts. Work 1 rnd even. Rep last 2 rnds, working 2 less k sts between dec's, 2 (3, 4) times more—8 sts. Cut yarn and pull through rem sts. Draw up tightly to secure. Fasten off.

WOVEN SCARF
Winter weave

Designer **Chris Bylsma** weaves style into winter with this scarf using warp and weft instead of knit and purl. A broad stripe down the middle incorporates a touch of rust and is accented by a finer weave on either side.

KNITTED MEASUREMENTS
- Approx 6"x67"/15x170cm (with fringe)

MATERIALS
- 2 3½oz/100g balls (each approx 132yd/121m) of Cascade Yarns *Pastaza* (wool) in #033 med blue (MC) (5)
- 1 ball each in #016 navy (A), #062 rust (B) and #031 light blue (C)
- One pair size 10½ (6.5mm) needles *or size to obtain gauge*
- Foam core board
- Quilting pins

GAUGE
13 sts and 22 rows to 4"/10cm over seed st using size 10½ (6.5mm) needles.
Take time to check gauge.

WEAVING PATTERN
With A, weave 1 strand over and under 1 ladder at a time. Rep 3 times more.
With MC, weave 2 strands together over and under 2 ladders at a time.
With B, weave 2 strands together over and under 2 ladders at a time.

With MC, weave 2 strands together over and under 2 ladders at a time.
With C, weave 3 strands together over and under 3 ladders at a time. Rep twice more.
With MC, weave 2 strands together over and under 2 ladders at a time.
With B, weave 2 strands together over and under 2 ladders at a time.
With MC, weave 2 strands together over and under 2 ladders at a time.
With A, weave 1 strand over and under 1 ladder at a time. Rep 3 times more.

SCARF
With MC, using double cast-on method, cast on 10 sts. **Row I (RS)** K1, p1, k6, p1, k1. **Row 2** K1, p1, k1, p4, k1, p1, k1. Rep last 2 rows until piece measures 60"/152cm from beg. You will be creating a St st channel with seed st on either side. **Note** The scarf will appear narrow and distorted until you drop sts and weave.
Bind off row
Bind off 2 sts. With 1 st on RH needle, drop the 4 sts in St st and unravel all the way to and through the bind off sts. Elongate the st on the RH needle to bridge the gap created by the dropped sts (approx 4-5"/10-12cm long). Take the tension off the carrying yarn and bind off the elongated st without tightening the st or the carrying yarn. The bind off across the dropped sts must be the same width as the dropped st channel. Cont to bind off all rem sts.

KNIT WEAVING

Cut lengths of yarn for weaving, 20"/ 51cm longer than scarf, as foll: 8 strands A, 4 strands B, 9 strands C, 8 strands MC. Pin the scarf along each edge of the dropped st channel onto foam core boards (the entire length of the scarf must be pinned from one end to the other). Place pins about 1"/2.5cm apart to keep the channel taut.

Foll weaving pat, using a tapestry needle to weave the cut strands under and over the ladders. Pull the yarn through from one end to the other, leaving tails approx same length at each end. Tug the yarns to the side after weaving each one (a pick comb or tip of knitting needle work well).

FRINGE

Remove the scarf from the foam core and adjust the tension of the weaving yarns as needed. Beg at outside edges and working into center, knot 4 strands of weaving yarn tails at a time with overhead knots. Knot the remaining 5 center strands into one knot. Rep for the other end. For outer edge fringe, cut 16 lengths of MC, 20"/51cm long. Pull 2 strands at a time half way through an edge st and knot into an overhand knot. Add a total of 4 fringe knots on each end, tying in the cast-on and bound-off tails with the edge knots. Trim all fringe to 7"/18cm long.

HAT WITH EARFLAPS
Candy stripes

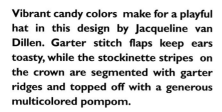

Vibrant candy colors make for a playful hat in this design by Jacqueline van Dillen. Garter stitch flaps keep ears toasty, while the stockinette stripes on the crown are segmented with garter ridges and topped off with a generous multicolored pompom.

SIZES

One size fits all. This hat is a loose fitting style.

KNITTED MEASUREMENTS

- Head circumference approx 21"/53cm
- Depth 11"/28cm

MATERIALS

- 2 1¾oz/50g balls (each approx 55yd/50m) of Berroco, Inc. *Pronto* (cotton/acrylic) in #4483 pink (A) (5)
- 1 ball each in #4463 white (B), #4400 orange (C) and #4440 dk pink (D)
- One pair size 9 (5.5mm) needles *or size to obtain gauge*
- Size I/9 (5.5mm) crochet hook

GAUGE

15 sts and 22 rows to 4"/10cm over St st using size 9 (5.5mm) needles.
Take time to check gauge.

HAT

With D, cast on 86 sts. K 4 rows. Change to A. **Next row (RS)** K1, *k26, k2tog; rep from * to last st, k1. Work 3 rows even. Rep last 4 rows twice more, working 1 less k st between decs every dec row—77 sts. Change to D. K 2 rows. Change to B. **Next row (RS)** K1, *k23, k2tog; rep from * to last st, k1. Work 3 rows even. Rep last 4 rows twice more, working 1 less k st between decs every dec row—68 sts. Change to D. K 2 rows. Change to C. **Next row (RS)** K1, *k20, k2tog; rep from * to last st, k1. Work 3 rows even. Rep last 4 rows twice more, working 1 less k st between decs every dec row—59 sts. Change to D. K 2 rows. Change to A. **Next row (RS)** K1, k2tog, *k7, k2tog; rep from * to last 2 sts, k2tog. Work 3 rows even. Rep last 4 rows twice more, working 1 less k st between decs every dec row—35 sts. Change to D. K 2 rows. Change to B. **Next row (RS)** K1, k2tog, *k4, k2tog; rep from * to last 2 sts, k2tog. Work 3 rows even. Rep last 4 rows twice more, working 1 less k st between decs every dec row—14 sts. **Next row (RS)** K2tog across—7 sts.

Cut yarn, leaving a long tail for sewing seam. Draw through rem sts and fasten tightly. Sew back seam.

Ear flaps

With WS facing and B, pick up and k16

sts, beg 2½"/6.5cm from back seam. **Note** Read foll instructions before beg to work. Working in garter st, work stripe pat as foll: *2 rows B, 2 rows C, 2 rows B, 2 rows A; rep from * twice more, work 2 rows B, AT SAME TIME, dec 1 st each side every other row beg with 2nd B stripe—4 sts and 26 rows. Bind off. Work a 2nd ear flap in same way along other side of back seam.

FINISHING

With RS facing, crochet hook and D, work 1 rnd sc around lower edge and ear flaps. With 2 strands of D held tog, make 4 braids approx 5"/12.5cm long and attach to ends of ear flaps.

With all colors held tog, make 3"/7.5cm pompom. Attach to top of hat.

The ultra-long skinny scarf, designed by Miriam Gold, is back in fine form and, combined with chunky yarn, it's a swift and au courant project. Knit in garter stitch and finished with vibrant variegated fringe, the look is pulled together with a stockinette stitch cap, designed by Joanne Yordanou, using the same bright multicolored yarn and topped with a tassel.

SIZES
Cap
One size fits all. This cap is a loose fitting style.

KNITTED MEASUREMENTS
Cap
- Head circumference 21"/53.5cm
- Depth 8"/20.5cm
Scarf
- Approx 4" x 84"/10 x 213cm (without fringe)

MATERIALS
Cap
- 2 3½oz/100g balls (each approx 33yd/30m) of Rowan *Biggy Print* (wool) in #255 pink multi (A) **(6)**
- 1 3½oz/100g ball (each approx 86yd/80m) of Rowan *Big Wool* (wool) in #10 blue (B) **(5)**
- One pair size 35 (19mm) needles *or size to obtain gauge*
Scarf
- 2 balls of Rowan *Big Wool* in #10 blue (B)

- 1 ball of Rowan *Biggy Print* in #255 pink multi (A)
- One pair size 15 (10mm) needles *or size to obtain gauge*

GAUGES
Cap
5.5 sts and 7 rows to 4"/10cm over St st using size 35 (19mm) needles.
Scarf
10 sts and 16 rows to 4"/10cm over garter st using size 15 (10mm) needles.
Take time to check gauges.

CAP
With A, cast on 29 sts. **Row I (WS)** Knit. **Row 2** Purl. **Row 3** Purl. **Row 4** Knit. Beg with a k row, work in St st until piece measures 6"/15cm from beg.
Shape top
Next row (RS) K1, *k2tog, k2; rep from * to end—22 sts. **Next row** P1, *p2tog, p1; rep from * to end—15 sts. **Next row** K1, *k2tog; rep from * to end—8 sts. **Next row** P2tog across—4 sts.
Cut yarn and thread through rem sts. Fasten top. Sew seam.
Tassel
With B, make tassel, leaving a 6"/15cm tail. Secure to top of hat.

SCARF
With B, cast on 10 sts. Work in garter stitch for 84"/213cm. Bind off.
Fringe
With A, cut 68"/172.5cm lengths. Attach fringe to every other st at each edge.

RUFFLED EDGE SCARF

Strawberry shortcake

Add a flourish to the basic ribbed scarf with this design from Michelle Woodford. Continuing in a rib but using a series of increases, each end flowers into a broad scalloped ruffle for a bit of flair.

KNITTED MEASUREMENTS

- Approx 6½" x 68"/16.5 x 172.5cm

MATERIALS

- 8 1¾oz/50g balls (each approx 55yd/50m) of DiVé/LBUSA *Fiamma* (wool) in #24007 red (**5**)
- One pair size 11 (8mm) needles *or size to obtain gauge*

GAUGE

12 sts and 15 rows to 4"/10cm over k2, p2 rib (slightly stretched) using size 11 (8mm) needles.
Take time to check gauge.

STITCH GLOSSARY

L-inc With tip of LH needle, lift and k the left loop of the st below the st just knit on RH needle.
R-inc With tip of RH needle, lift and k the right loop of the st below the st just knit on LH needle.

SCARF

Cast on 90 sts. Work in rib as foll: **Row 1 (WS)** *P6, k6; rep from *, end p6. **Row 2** *K6, p6; rep from *, end k6. Rep last 2 rows 3 times more, then work row 1 once more. **Next (dec) row (RS)** *Ssk, k2, k2tog, p6; rep from * to last 6 sts, ssk, k2, k2tog—74 sts. **Next (dec) row (WS)** *P4, ssk, k2, k2tog; rep from *, end p4—60 sts. Work even in k4, p4 rib for 8 rows more. **Next (dec) row (RS)** *Ssk, k2tog, p4; rep from * to last 4 sts, ssk, k2tog—44 sts. **Next (dec) row (WS)** *P2, ssk, k2tog; rep from *, end p2—30 sts. **Next row (RS)** *K2, p2; rep from *, end k2. Work even in k2, p2 rib until piece measures 62"/157.5cm from beg, end with a WS row.

Next (inc ruffle) row (RS) *K1, L-inc, R-inc, k1, p2; rep from *, end k1, L-inc, R-inc, k1—46 sts. **Next (inc ruffle) row (WS)** *P4, k1, L-inc, R-inc, k1; rep from *, end p4—60 sts. Work even in k4, p4 rib for 8 rows more **Next (inc) row (RS)** *K1, L-inc, k2, R-inc, k1, p4; rep from *, end k1, L-inc, k2, R-inc, k1— 76 sts. **Next (inc) row (WS)** *P6, k1, L-inc, k2, R-inc, k1; rep from *, end p6—90 sts. Work even in k6, p6 rib for 8 rows more. Bind off in pat.

■■■▭

Michelle Woodford uses soft tones of blue and brown to create a playful tasseled hat. Thick, spiraling cables adorn this cone-shaped style, diminishing in size to meet at its top point.

SIZES

Instructions are written for Child's size X-Small. Changes for Child's through adult unisex Small, Medium, Large, X-Large are in parentheses. This hat is a close-fitting style.

KNITTED MEASUREMENTS

■ Head circumference 12 (14, 16, 18, 20)"/30.5 (35.5, 40.5, 45.5, 50.5)cm
■ Depth approx 9 (9, 11, 11, 11½)"/23 (23, 28, 28, 29) cm

MATERIALS

■ 1 3½oz/100g ball (each approx 100yd/90m) of Crystal Palace *Iceland* (wool) each in #7063 blue (MC) and #3433 bark (A) (**5**)
■ One set (4) size 11 (8mm) needles *or size to obtain gauge*
■ Size L/11 (8mm) crochet hook
■ Cable needle
■ Stitch markers

GAUGE

14 sts and 14 rows to 4"/10cm over cable pat using size 11 (8mm) needles.
Take time to check gauge.

STITCH GLOSSARY

6-St RC Sl 3 sts to cn and hold to *back*, k3, k3 from cn.

6-St dec RC Sl 3 sts to cn and hold to *back*, k1, k2tog; then work ssk, k1 from cn.

4-St RC Sl 2 sts to cn and hold to *back*, k2, k2 from cn.

4-St dec RC Sl 2 sts to cn and hold to *back*, k2tog; then work ssk from cn.

HAT

With MC, cast on 42 (49, 56, 63, 70) sts. Divide sts evenly over 3 needles. Pm and join, being careful not to twist sts.

Rnd 1 (RS) *P1, k6; rep from * to end.

Rnds 2-5 K the knit and p the purl sts.

Rnd 6 *P1, 6-st RC; rep from * to end.

Rnds 7-13 K the knit and p the purl sts.

Rnd 14 Rep rnd 6.

Rnds 15-19 K the knit and p the purl sts.

Rnd 20 (dec rnd) *P1, 6-st dec RC; rep from * around—30 (35, 40, 45, 50) sts.

Rnds 21-25 K the knit and p the purl sts.

Rnd 26 (sizes Medium, Large, X-Large only) *P1, 4-st RC; rep from * around.

Rnds 27-29 (sizes Medium, Large, X-Large only) K the knit and p the purl sts.

Rnd 30 (dec rnd for all sizes) *P1, 4-st dec RC; rep from * around—18 (21, 24, 27, 30) sts. Work even for 3 (3, 5, 5, 6) rnds more.

Next dec rnd *P1, k2tog twice; rep from *around—6 (7, 8, 9, 10) sts. Cont to k2tog around until there are 4 sts.

FINISHING

Cut yarn and pull through rem sts. Draw up tightly to secure. Fasten off.

I-cord edging

With RS facing, dpn and CC, pick up and k 1 st in each cast-on st around lower edge. With CC and 2nd dpn, cast on 3 sts. **Rnd 1** *K2, sl 1, k1 from picked up edge of hat, psso to join I-cord to edge. Slide sts to beg of same dpn; rep from * until all sts are worked. Bind off. Sew cast-on and bound-off edges of I-cord tog.

Tassel

With MC and A, make 6"/15cm long tassel.

With MC, and crochet hook, chain 2"/5cm. Attach to top of hat, then attach tassel to end of chain.

On the fringe

This burgundy and lavender concoction designed by Debbie Fein breaks all the rules. A basic wool is worked in a two/two rib, while strands of shiny purple chenille are sewn into place. A striking combination of contrasting texture and color.

KNITTED MEASUREMENTS
- Approx 11½" x 98"/29 x 249cm

MATERIALS
- 9   1¾oz/50g balls (each approx 62yd/57m) of GGH/Muench Yarns *Aspen* (wool/acrylic) in #5 burgundy (A) (⑤)
- 4   1¾oz/50g balls (each approx 61yd/56m) of Muench Yarns *Touch Me* (viscose/wool) in #3645 lilac (B) (⑤)
- One pair size 11 (8mm) needles *or size to obtain gauge*

GAUGE
11 sts and 14 rows to 4"/10cm over k2, p2 rib (slightly stretched) using size 11 (8mm) needles.
Take time to check gauge.

Notes
1 The st count is increased on rows 2 and 10, and restored on rows 8 and 16 when yo's are dropped.
2 Allow dropped yo's to unravel, forming a medallion that will later be woven with strands of B.

STITCH PATTERN
(over 32 sts)
Row 1 (WS) P1, [k2, p2] 7 times, k2, p1.
Row 2 K1, [p2, k1, yo, k1, p2, k2] 3 times, p2, k1, yo, k1, p2, k1—36 sts.
Row 3 P1, [k2, p3, k2, p2] 3 times, k2, p3, k2, p1.
Row 4 K1, [p2, k3, p2, k2] 3 times, p2, k3, p2, k1.
Row 5 Rep row 3.
Row 6 Rep row 4.
Row 7 Rep row 3.
Row 8 K1, [p2, k1, drop 1, k1, p2, k2] 3 times, p2, k1, drop 1, k1, p2, k1—32 sts.
Row 9 Rep row 1.
Row 10 K1, [p2, k2, p2, k1, yo, k1] 3 times, p2, k2, p2, k1—35 sts.
Row 11 P1, [k2, p2, k2, p3] 3 times, k2, p2, k2, p1.
Row 12 K1, [p2, k2, p2, k3] 3 times, p2, k2, p2, k1.
Row 13 Rep row 11.
Row 14 Rep row 12.
Row 15 Rep row 11.
Row 16 K1, [p2, k2, p2, k1, drop 1, k1] 3 times, p2, k2, p2, k1—32 sts.
Rep these 16 rows for st pat.

SCARF
With A, cast on 32 sts. Work 16 rows in st

pat for approx 98"/249cm, end with a pat row 1 or 9. Bind off.

FINISHING

Block piece to measurements.

Cut a 60"/152cm long strand of B. Beg with medallion at one end of scarf, weave the strand of B [under, over] 3 times, and under the 7 strands of A. Leaving approx 5½"/14cm tails on both ends, cut B. Weave the 2nd strand next to the first, weaving [over, under] 3 times, and over. Leaving approx 5½"/14cm tails on both ends, cut B. Rep weaving process for 5 strands of B (2 full rep of weaving pat, end [under, over] 3 times). Double knot both ends of strands 2 and 4 over strands 1, 3, and 5 to secure. Rep until all medallions are woven. When weaving medallions at the short ends of scarf, leave 12"/30.5cm long tails to create fringe.

How about a little whim for the winter? Kathy Sasser's critter scarf is completely unique and completely simple to make. Stockinette stitch and garter stitch make up the thirty-legged body, while the narrow width is perfect for a child's neck.

KNITTED MEASUREMENTS
■ Approx 4½" x 45"/11.5 x 114cm

MATERIALS
■ 2 3½oz/100g balls (each approx 200yd/182m) each of Plymouth Yarn *Encore* (acrylic/wool) in #1014 yellow (A) and #1204 lt brown (B) (4)
■ One pair size 10 (6mm) needles *or size to obtain gauge*
■ Two size 10 (6mm) dpn

GAUGE
13 sts and 18 rows to 4"/10cm over St st using size 10 (6mm) needles and 2 strands of yarn held tog.
Take time to check gauge.

Note
Use 2 strands of yarn held tog throughout.

SCARF
Beg tail
With A, cast on 2 sts. **Row 1 (RS)** K1, M1, k1—3 sts. **Row 2** Purl. **Row 3** K1, M1, k1, M1, k1—5 sts. **Row 4** Purl. **Row 5** K1, M1, work to last st, M1, k1—7 sts. **Row 6** Purl. Cont in this way to dec 1 st each side every RS row 4 times more—15

sts. *Change to B, work in garter st for 4 rows. Change to A, work in St st for 8 rows*; rep between *'s 13 times more. Change to B, work in garter st for 4 rows.
Beg head
Change to A, work in St st for 10 rows. **Next row (RS)** K1, M1, work to last st, M1, k1—17 sts. Work 3 rows even. **Next row (RS)** K1, M1, work to last st, M1, k1—19 sts. Work 5 rows even. **Next row (RS)** K1, ssk, work to last 3 sts, k2tog, k1—17 sts. Work 3 rows even. **Next row (RS)** K1, ssk, work to last 3 sts, k2tog, k1—15 sts. Work 1 row even. Rep last 2 rows 4 times more—7 sts. Bind off.

FINISHING
Block piece to measurements.
Legs
With RS facing, dpn and A, pick up 3 sts along side edge of brown garter stripe. Work I-cord as foll: *Slide sts to beg of needle and k3, pulling yarn firmly; rep from * until leg measures 2"/5cm. Bind off.
Rep for 30 legs, 1 along each side of brown garter stripes.
Antenna
(make 2)
With dpn and B, cast on 3 sts. Work between *'s for legs until I-cord measures 10"/25.5cm. Bind off. Sew to head as in photo.
With B, duplicate st eyes and mouth as in photo.

Wendy Henderson infuses her ribbed scarf with a dash of spring color in this charming style. With an earthy green background and lovely purple flowers, you can remind yourself every day that warm weather is on the way.

KNITTED MEASUREMENTS
■ Approx 8" x 72"/20.5 x 183cm

MATERIALS
■ 3 3½oz/100g balls (each approx 60yd/54m) of Rowan Yarn *Polar* (wool/alpaca) in #644 green (MC) 💶

■ 1 ball in #650 pale lilac (A)

■ 1 1¾oz/50g ball (each approx 219yd/200m) of Rowan Yarn *Rowanspun* (wool) in #746 lilac (B) 💶

■ 1 .88oz/25g ball (each approx 229yd/210m) of Rowan Yarn *Kidsilk Haze* (mohair/silk) in #600 purple (C) 💶

■ One pair size 13 (9mm) needles or *size to obtain gauge*

GAUGE
16 sts and 14 rows to 4"/10cm over pat st using MC and size 13 (9mm) needles.
Take time to check gauge.

PATTERN STITCH
(multiple of 6 sts plus 3)
Row 1 (RS) K3, *p3, k3; rep from * to end.
Row 2 P1, *k1, p1; rep from * to end.
Rep rows 1 and 2 for pat st.

Note
When working flowers, use 2 strands B held tog and 3 strands C held tog.

SCARF
With MC, cast on 27 sts. Work in pat st for 72"/183cm from beg. Bind off.

FLOWERS
(make 2 each in A, B and C)
Cast on 56 sts.
Row 1 (RS) Knit.
Row 2 P2tog across—28 sts.
Row 3 Knit.
Row 4 Purl.
Row 5 K2tog across—14 sts.
Row 6 Purl.
Row 7 K2tog across—7 sts.
Cut yarn, leaving 15"/38cm tail. Draw through rem sts and fasten. Sew edges together, allow outer edge to curl inward.

FLOWER CENTER (BOBBLE)
(Make 6 in MC)
Cast on 1 st, leaving 15"/38cm tail after cast on.
Row 1 (RS) K into front, back, front, back, front of st—5 sts.
Row 2 Purl.
Row 3 K1, SK2P, k1—3 sts.
Row 4 P3tog—1 st.
Cut yarn, leaving 15"/38cm tail. Fasten st.

FINISHING
Place bobble in center of flower. Pull the 2 ends through flower and tie a knot on WS. Place flower on scarf in desired position. Pull 2 ends of bobble through scarf and tie a knot on WS. Rep for other flowers, attaching 3 flowers to each end of scarf.

Bonnie Franz's racer stripe-inspired scarf is a menswear classic. Worked in garter stitch in full-length rows, this beautiful basic gives the effect of simultaneous vertical and horizontal striping.

KNITTED MEASUREMENTS
Approx 6" x 62"/15 x 157.5cm

MATERIALS
3 1¾oz/50g balls (each approx 60yd/54m) of Lion Brand Yarn Company *Kool Wool* (acrylic/wool) in #113 red (MC) (5️⃣)

1 ball each in #149 grey (A) and #153 black (B)

Size 10½ (6.5mm) circular needle 32"/80cm *or size to obtain gauge*

GAUGE
12 sts and 20 rows to 4"/10cm over garter st using size 10½ (6.5mm) needles.
Take time to check gauge.

Notes
1 Scarf is worked horizontally.
2 Circular needle is used to accommodate the large number of sts. Work back and forth in rows.

SCARF
With MC, cast on 180 sts. Work in garter st and stripe pat as foll: work 10 rows MC, 4 rows A, 2 rows B, 4 rows A, 10 rows MC. Bind off in MC.

A traditional Turkish design is the starting point for this captivating hat. Marrying pink and hues, Mary de Bruyn uses garter stitch for the border and a slip-stitch mosaic pattern for the crown to create a design that works day to night.

SIZES
One size fits all. This hat is a loose-fitting style.

KNITTED MEASUREMENTS
- Head circumference 20"/51cm
- Depth 8"/20.5cm

MATERIALS
- 1 3½oz/100g ball each (each approx 82yd/75m) of Debbie Bliss *Cashmerino Super Chunky* (wool/microfiber/ cashmere) in #03 dk plum (A) and #02 pink (B) **⑤**
- One set (4) size 10½ (6.5mm) dpn or size *to obtain gauge*
- Stitch markers

GAUGE
13 sts and 21 rows to 4"/10cm over sl st pat using size 10½ (6.5mm) dpn.
Take time to check gauge.

SLIP STITCH PATTERN
(multiple of 14 sts)
Rnd 1 With A, *k1, sl 1, k3, sl 1, k1; rep from * around.
Rnd 2 and all even rnds With color used in previous rnd, k the knit sts and sl the slipped sts.
Rnd 3 With B, *sl 1, k3, sl 1, k4, sl 1, k3, sl 1; rep from * around.
Rnd 5 With A, *k3, sl 1, k3; rep from * around.
Rnd 7 With B, *k2, sl 1, k3, sl 2, k3, sl 1, k2; rep from * around.
Rnd 8 Rep rnd 2.
Rep rnds 1-8 for sl st pat.

Notes
1 When working sl st pat, always sl sts purlwise with yarn in back.
2 Work garter st in the rnd as foll: *k 1 rnd, p 1 rnd; rep from * for garter st in the rnd.

HAT
With A, cast on 70 sts. Divide over 3 dpn as foll: 23 sts on 1st needle, 23 sts on 2nd needle, 24 sts on 3rd needle. Pm and join, taking care not to twists st on needle. P 1 rnd with A. Then work garter st band as foll: 2 rnds B, 2 rnds A, 2 rnds B. Work rnds 1-8 of sl st pat once, then work rnds 1-6 once more. Then beg with rnd 3, work sl st pat in reverse as foll: work rnds 3-1, then cont to rep rnds 8-1 until 30 rnds of sl st pat have been worked above garter st band.

Shape crown
Next (dec) rnd *Work 5 sts in pat, k2tog, ssk, work 5 sts in pat; rep from * to end— 60 sts.
Work 1 rnd even.
Next (dec) rnd *Work 4 sts in pat, k2tog,

ssk, work 4 sts in pat; rep from * to end—50 sts.

Work 1 rnd even.

Next (dec) rnd Work 3 sts in pat, k2tog, ssk, work 3 sts in pat; rep from * to end—40 sts.

Work 1 rnd even.

Next (dec) rnd *Work 2 sts in pat, k2tog, ssk, work 2 sts in pat; rep from * to end—30 sts.

Work 1 rnd even.

Next (dec) rnd *Work 1 st in pat, k2tog, ssk, work 1 st in pat; rep from * to end—20 sts.

Work 1 rnd even.

Next (dec) rnd *K2tog, ssk; rep from * to end—10 sts.

Cut yarn. Draw through rem sts and fasten tightly.

GARTER HAT
Going loopy

■■■□

Song Palmese's short row wrapping gives this variegated purple and red hat a whole new look and a great fit. The added detail of dropped stitch fringe infuses the pattern with a merry and quirky appeal.

SIZES
One size fits all. This cap is a loose-fitting style.

KNITTED MEASUREMENTS
- Head circumference 19"/48cm
- Depth 8½"/21.5cm

MATERIALS
- 3 1¾oz/50g balls (each approx 50yd/45m) of GGH/Muench Yarns *Sierra* (wool/nylon) in #10 pink multi ⑤
- One pair size 13 (9mm) needles *or size to obtain gauge*

GAUGE
10 sts and 21 rows to 4"/10cm over garter st using size 13 (9mm) needles.
Take time to check gauge.

SHORT ROW WRAPPING
(wrap and turn - w&t)
Knit side
1 Wyib, sl next st purlwise.
2 Move yarn between the needles to the front.
3 Sl the same st back to LH needle. Turn work, bring yarn to the p side between needles. One st is wrapped. When short rows are completed, work to just before wrapped st, insert RH needle under the wrap and knitwise into the wrapped st, k them tog.

STITCH PATTERN
Row 1 (WS) K19, p1, k to end.
Row 2 K6, sl 1, k to 2 sts from end, w&t.
Row 3 and all WS rows K to 7 sts from end, p1, k to end.
Row 4 K6, sl 1, k to 4 sts from end, w&t.
Row 6 K6, sl 1, k to 6 sts from end, w&t.
Row 8 K6, sl 1, k to 8 sts from end, w&t.
Row 10 K6, sl 1, k to 6 sts from end, w&t.
Row 12 K6, sl 1, k to 4 sts from end, w&t.
Row 14 K6, sl 1, k to 2 sts from end, w&t.
Row 16 K6, sl 1, k to end.
Rep these 16 rows for stitch pat.

With waste yarn and using provisional cast on (see page 16), cast on 26 sts. Change to working yarn. Work 16 rows of st pat 6 times. Work row 1 once more. Cut yarn, leaving 30"/76cm tail for grafting.

FINISHING

Drop last 2 sts off needle and let them hang. Undo waste yarn holding first row of knitting. Using Kitcheners stitch, graft last row of knitting to first row. Sew gap at top of hat closed.

Brim

Unravel all rows of dropped sts and tie each loop with an overhand knot close to knitting to finish fringe. Fold brim at sl st row.

NOTES

NOTES

RESOURCES

US RESOURCES

Write to the yarn companies listed below for purchasing and mail-order information.

ANNY BLATT
7796 Boardwalk
Brighton, MI 48116

ARTFUL YARNS
distributed by
JCA, Inc.

BERROCO, INC.
P.O. Box 367
Uxbridge, MA 01569

BROWN SHEEP CO.
100662 County Road 16
Mitchell, NE 69357

CASCADE YARNS
1224 Andover Park E.
Tukwila, WA 98188-3950
(800) 548-1048

CLASSIC ELITE YARNS
300 Jackson Street, Bldg. #5
Lowell, MA 01852

CRYSTAL PALACE
2340 Bissell Avenue
Richmond, CA 94804
www.straw.com

COLINETTE YARNS
distributed by
Unique Kolours

DESIGNS BY JUDITH
P.O. Box 770
Medford, MA 02155

DEBBIE BLISS
distributed by KFI

DIVÉ
distributed by
LBUSA

FIESTA YARNS
206 Frontage Road
Rio Rancho, NM 87124

GGH
distributed by
Muench Yarns

GEDIFRA
distributed by KFI

JCA, INC.
35 Scales Lane
Townsend, MA 01469

KFI
P.O. Box 502
Roosevelt, NY 11575

LBUSA
P.O. Box 217
Colorado Springs, CO 80901

LION BRAND YARN CO.
34 West 15th Street
New York, NY 10011

MANOS DEL URUGUAY
distributed by
Designs by Judith

MUENCH YARNS
285 Bel Marin Keys Blvd.
Unit J
Novato, CA 94949-5724
muenchyarn.aol.com

PATON® YARNS
P.O. Box 40
Listowel, ON N4W3H3

PLYMOUTH YARN
P.O. Box 28
Bristol, PA 19007

ROWAN YARNS
4 Townsend West, Unit 8
Nashua, NH 03063

SKACEL COLLECTION, INC.
P.O. Box 88110
Seattle, WA 98138-2110

TAHKI YARNS
distributed by
Tahki•Stacy Charles, Inc.

TAHKI•STACY CHARLES, INC.
8000 Cooper Ave.
Bldg. 1, 3rd floor
Glendale, NY 11385

UNIQUE KOLOURS
1428 Oak Lane
Downingtown, PA 19335

CANADIAN RESOURCES

Write to US resources for mail-order availability of yarns not listed.

BERROCO, INC.
distributed by
S. R. Kertzer, Ltd.

CLASSIC ELITE YARNS
distributed by

S. R. Kertzer, Ltd.

DIAMOND YARN
9697 St. Laurent
Montreal, PQ H3L 2N1
and
155 Martin Ross, Unit #3
Toronto, ON M3J 2L9

LES FILS MUENCH, CANADA
5640 rue Valcourt
Brossard, PQ

J4W 1C5 Canada

MUENCH YARNS, INC.
distributed by
Les Fils Muench, Canada

PATONS®
PO Box 40
Listowel, ON N4W 3H3

ROWAN YARNS
distributed by
Diamond Yarn

UK RESOURCES

Not all yarns used in this book are available in the UK. For yarns not available, make a comparable substitute or contact the US manufacturer for purchasing and mail-order information.

ROWAN YARNS
Green Lane Mill
Holmfirth
West Yorks HD7 1RW
Tel: 01484-681881

SILKSTONE
12 Market Place
Cockermouth
Cumbria, CA13 9NQ
Tel: 01900-821052

THOMAS RAMSDEN GROUP
Netherfield Road
Guiseley
West Yorks LS20 9PD
Tel: 01943-872264

Editorial Director
TRISHA MALCOLM

Art Director
CHI LING MOY

Executive Editor
CARLA S. SCOTT

Instructions Editor
KAREN GREENWALD

Yarn Editor
VERONICA MANNO

Assistant Editor
MIRIAM GOLD
JEAN GUIRGUIS

Graphic Designer
CAROLINE WONG

Stylist
LAURA MAFFEO

Book Manager
MICHELLE LO

Production Manager
DAVID JOINNIDES

Photography
QUENET STUDIOS

Photo Stylist
LAURA MAFFEO

President, Sixth&Spring Books
ART JOINNIDES

LOOK FOR THESE OTHER TITLES IN
THE *VOGUE KNITTING ON THE GO!* SERIES...

BABY BLANKETS

BABY GIFTS

BABY KNITS

BABY KNITS TWO

BAGS & BACKPACKS

BEGINNER BASICS

CAPS & HATS

CAPS & HATS TWO

CHUNKY KNITS

CROCHETED SCARVES

KIDS KNITS

MITTENS & GLOVES

PILLOWS

SCARVES

SCARVES TWO

SOCKS

SOCKS TWO

TEEN KNITS

TODDLER KNITS

VESTS

VINTAGE KNITS

WEEKEND KNITS